IDENTITY

An opus of evolution

C.T. FINNEY

Contents

A Foreword from the Author

The concept of identity is one that has always been incredibly fascinating to me. So fascinating in fact, that my obsession with it occupied the last five years of my life. Each year that passed, I would always think *okay, you're done with identity now—move on to another topic and put the past to rest.*

But the past is never really laid to rest until its damn well ready to lie down, and the contents of this book—each poem like a black and white frame of a timestamp—prove that fact to be true, to me. In that way, I suppose I think of this work (a labor of childbirth that took half a decade to deliver) as my own "growing up" story. And each poem, in itself, is a growing pain that I still remember.

In that sense, it is an opus of a metaphysical evolution of what it's like to be inside the mind as it undergoes a metamorphosis from the years of twenty to twenty-five. I maintain that these years are harsh and most twenty to twenty-five-year-olds aren't credited for the existential crisis that they begin to experience—everyone told us to follow our dreams, yet no one gave us a road map or manual of how to get there and work through the problems ourselves.

It's at that magical age where one begins to really think about who they are as an individual and what they truly value as opposed to what their impulses taught them to value in the years prior. Because my mind functions as an artist, I cannot help but creatively romanticize the moments that I experienced, and the questions I sought answers to that served as the catalyst for this period of change for me.

It is the discrepancy that we actually notice between the gap of where we are currently and where we want to be

● ● ●

3

that causes the mid-youth crisis. As that is the case, we grow from that experience and it took me five years to find out that this concept is what actually solidifies our identity; that we faced hell and battled our own bodies in order to take control over what we are and master ourselves in order to navigate us to where we want to be.

The contents of this book can be summed up in one simple phrase; it is an exorcism of the past through confession of the present in order to sanctify a future. The book is divided into three sections, or for me—three major periods of my life—*In Transit, Identity, and Darker Shades of Glam*. Each section is a proper requiem to the questions I now have answers for and it is the written treaty of peace that I have made with myself over the things I could not control.

In Transit exists as the exposition where I first began noticing my place in the universe. That awareness began by first developing an awareness of what was around me; nature, energy, and other themes pervade the epicenter of myself—that is the point where I first noticed that everything was in motion; in a perpetual state of movement and that I had two options: move. Or remain where I stood and be swallowed by it all.

Identity explores the facet of my personal quest to discover who I am. It is a reexamination of my past experiences in order to investigate them, meditate on them, and determine how the events of the past molded the contour of who I am—how I react, what I say, and how I think.

Darker Shades of Glam is specifically about another aspect of identity—it is the impact of influence and how influence contributes to who we become. It is as much about the exposure to people we associate with as well as the impressions of art that we take into our being. A lot of the pieces in *Darker Shades of Glam* are tributes, or odes, to people, poets, and works of art who have had the most effect on me.

As the book moves forward, it is my hope that those who read it can find a solace in my words; that what is written will pervade the sense of consciousness and awake others, like myself, into self-awareness. And as for those readers who are already self-aware, it is my hope that this book nourishes your emotions and can serve as the gateway to nostalgia, through which you can travel to remember. And that concept: memory, is what this book is all about.

-C.T. Finney

IDENTITY

An opus of evolution

A WORK OF METAMORPHOSIS BY:

C.T. FINNEY

I

IN TRANSIT

The Wildwoods

In the embrace of the Blue Ridge,
my cradle of origin,
the shadow of the day
sweeps across the foothills—

green foliage rolling its eyes;
a smile's edge is luminescence
in the dark. I wanted to deny
the wildwoods, clip off the vines
that wove their way within my being
just before the coarse whispers:

(*you'd be back,
I always knew it.*)

I am a wild-child, at heart
running naked in boundless space
where there is no distinction here
between eroded lines dividing
spheres of life and death. To we who live
within the murmuring pines
and whispering furs
this perpetual nascence is existence.

The Willow Tree

She hides her pain well, but
listen closer still:
in the creaks and groans
of the wind rolling through the willow's leaves,
twisting her branches, there is
a murmured agony;
her whispers to the shadows.

Ripples form her own reflection
in the troubled waters where
light stalks the illusion
of time's decay; her being,
evaporating.

She wonders where her friends
have gone

> *time has the habit*
> *of making constants disappear*

beach, ash, oak—
an axe in the dark.
elm, birch, maple—
sundered into planks, tempest lightning.

Too young for seedlings,
too old for regret;

> *I must survive,*
> *I must set the example.*

A Poetic Sketch on T'aoism

I could try to tell you
but you wouldn't understand;
people ask for an answer,

but it is not mine to give.
It is all about the simplicity of things—
the absolute zero.

Here is a gateway

connecting the understanding
of everything------>

        <------to the plane of knowing
           that you know nothing.

Fish My Mind for Compliments

for A. Champion

and there aren't any.
Material winds on breathless air:
where I am accused of flattery

but,
fish my mind for compliments

and you will find I speak
in only truths—
and those that are universal.

dreams of sunflowers

i planted a new seed the other day
just east of the mountains
and never being one
with a green thumb,
i still planted it anyway—

out of season and
i am reminded of the bamboo plant
that i murdered at sixteen.

yes it's true—some folks
should never be parents, but
i planted it anyway,

choosing land that had been scorched
from a lover's wildfire.

there, I saw a sunflower within a dream;
blooming bud, ruptured soil
in a hole that does not heal—life

is now in residence.
tangled veins
defy gravity outright;
roots in ash and earth,

its stalk through the
marrow of my bones
and a noose around my neck
make no mistake—

new seeds *can* grow
however unlikely
from the ashes
of what used to be, but

influence dies like a bad habit;
hard and rough and rotten to the core.

Rip-Tide

I took a trip to Mars
last night as I danced
along every blurred
and infinite line that
the rainbow-colored
cosmos drew.

I stood beyond time, tracing
kaleidoscopic eyes across
the shadowed face of God.

I have seen the exterior of
the mind of God in
a mound of trees that
grew at a mountain's summit.

The tissues were the leaves
glistening with oxygen and
every neuron was a firefly
firing off into each receptacle
as they thundered their way
up and down the mountain
of God's brain.

I discerned meaning when
a rip-tide rolled through my soul,
powerful enough to turn me
inside out as it drew my own
tears and used them
to wash me clean;

through brine-filled eyes,
a thought thunders above all:

be warned—I am capable
of falling in love now.

In Transit

At the bus stop, I acknowledge
that gravity has drawn me
to this one spot—speck on a map,
urban claustrophobia, where
time connects, the second hand
ceasing to tick; everything is
in perpetual motion.

that where I sit today,
was determined less
by my consciousness and more
by a choice of oatmeal
instead of cereal.

Everyone has some place to be, but
no one really knows
where they are going—not
here, not there,

caught somewhere in transit;

here is a matrix
of human suffering, where
we repeat lessons that we should
have learned long ago.

Everything Fades to Gray

I went to dance across
the face of the moon
and as time flew beyond
its infinite continuum, a
spectral hand appeared
and wrote a message; her
fingers were the pen and
the stars were her ink.

I saw her motion as she
drew the lines of oblivion and
told me to scramble for meaning
before it became lost.

I held fast to her left hand and
as she wrote the words that neither
eyes should see, nor ears
should hear; the rumbling muse of
my dark desire spoke
through the deep of the void,
the vibrations of her words resounding:

> *Truth has the property of being clear,*
> *while fallacy and frivolity fall into*
> *the muddy stream—*
>
> *there really is no black and white:*
> *everything just fades into gray.*

Supernova

Before I took my leave,
my old friends came to me with
questions. I would not tell them
answers in words, but in motions.

They knew me well and
interpreted my vibrations; imbibing
its raged splendor so
I could write out my answers like
a dying star, exploding in
one mighty supernova—

this was my farewell.

The curtain call comes
where shades of burgundy, burnt
orange, and amber
converge. I set my sail
into the universe. Nowhere
bound—rogue comet blazing
a trail into No Man's land where

growth is best obtained
by gravitating away from
the echoes of the past

II

IDENTITY

Words Unsung; confessions

The trade center crumbled into pieces, bringing America's dreams down with it. But to a ten-year old boy, sitting in class, struggling to form his *A's* and *E's* in cursive, watching all that dramatic press coverage on the TV that every teacher had tuned into and made their students watch, it didn't even seem like a big deal to him at all.

Nothing existed anyway, he knew that—because in the autumn of that year, his world had already been destroyed, and now he was trying so hard to feel and piece the fragments together one word at a time. He didn't know what "gay" was, or even what "lesbian" meant—he knew nothing of carnal desires, but what he did know was that this "lesbian" was responsible for shattering his world. Funny thing though, he didn't know which "lesbian" did it: his mom, or her lover. His heart raced, beating out of control as his lips trembled with words that went unsung.

It's true: his heart was broken, his happiness crushed as time suspended itself upon a string. He found he had to remind himself to breathe as his heart pounded at intervals; long strokes of solid divisions of pain in variable shades and confusing degrees. Everything became more difficult to do as he choked back tears and solemnly swore that he'd never hurt or cry again. He would deal with his parent's divorce on his own time.

Of Mothballs and Decay

There is a putrid smell
of mothballs and decay
wafting through my nostrils—

this is a childhood scene:
the arid weather of infernal southern
dog days, Bill Gaither blared through the radio
and the body began to mummify,
still—barely breathing.

He was dying then,
skin cancer would take him—but
I remember thin-blooded bruises
and crusted spots of decay better than most;

WWII dog tags jingle in the heat of the day,
where an illusion of grandeur is fostered.
When I was compelled
to do things a four year old shouldn't,
I thought of servicing a hero:
a withered finger moves to chapped lips,
a voice runs like the grain of sandpaper,

> *Shhh—Auntie Lou don't need to know,*
> *and don't nobody else neither.*

And so *nobody* never did,
then *everybody* wondered
why I didn't come around
to watch a corpse
smolder into a soiled mattress—

I told them I couldn't stand the smell
of mothballs. Being too strong,

it kept me away.

Spun

I.

I crashed to my knees
as the world spun around me
my body ached as I felt
the fever of chaos—
my higher self in communion
with me as it spoke through
the dark of my consciousness.
With religion forsaken, the only gods
I needed were my own ideologies.

I walked out into
the chilling October sky as
steam rose from my skin;
my bones clattered as I stood there singing:

October take me! October take me!

The anthem of my heart rose
in steady cadence as I
embraced the chill of
the early fall air—
I quaked in place for
a moment, my body
exorcised by the change
in the weather. The cosmos
reeled as the narrow beam of
reality upon which I walked
twisted and bent above the soaring
wings of time. Time is meaningless.
Time is meaningless. Meaning
is meaningless—

life threw itself out of balance as law
and plans gave way to anarchy
and spontaneity. It was then
that I realized: I could be anything
that I wanted to be.

II.

Glory to the pen!
Glory to the paper!
A mighty fortress is our art—
our song mingles with the movement
of receding childhood memories
briny drops of water trickle in
cascades around my face and nostalgia
shattered like a porcelain plate
dropped on hard linoleum
when I understood that my past was a lie—
faces flashed across an eye's horizon:
I held on to them for a fleeting moment
and then let them disappear
deleting memory after memory
from the archives of my brain—

the pig headed lover—
praise to him.
The rotting hand of my uncle, fondling
my balls in my dreams—
praise to him.
The melting faces of
my grandmother and aunts
and all the lies religion ever taught me—
praise to them.
The waning image of my mother's
disapproval or my father's
drunken stupors—praise be to them:

I'll wrap up the scattered ashes
of these people and places and
broken hearts and frowning faces
and after they've been razed
to the ground, I'll blow the ashes

● ● ●

into the wind.

III.

With my past forgiven,
the darkness of the night
embraced me. I yielded
myself to the shelter of
the unknown and with
the Milky Way as my playground,
I danced along the raging rings
of Saturn and reposed peacefully within
the storm of Jupiter's red eye.
My pupils contracted and expanded
to the size of the full moon in
all of its splendor as I realized:

I am awake—I am awake now;
I breathe, I feel, I see!
Darkness birthed in me
that which light forsook to overshadow.
I settled into my station as
the gravity of sociological precepts
crumbled into a fraction
of what it used to be and it lost
therein its meaning—

like a phoenix, I spread my wings
and burned away its influence,
cleansing my body of its poison.
My lips sprung forward in exile;
an exhalation to expel the remnants of its being
where the present is exorcised:

praise for the queer people! Praise for the freaks
that taught me variety is the nourishment of life!
Praise for the longitudes and latitudes
of adversity that birthed the strength in me

● ● ●

where once was weakness. For oppression
breathed into my ear and awoke my sense
of self, molded my shape, and breathed
life into the form of the image of the
beautiful creature that the present
now paints as me.

IV.

With the radiance of
the crown of thorns that adorned
my brow; ring of glory,
halo of liberation—my skin
became chicken hide as
the chill bumps of
the autumn wind raced
across my flesh;
stammering tongue swirling
with the southern swagger of
my vowels, cursing my name:

I am not who I think I am.
I am not who you think I am.
I am who I think that you think that I am—
a sail-seared wind in the sea of human life,
a vapor in a fleeting zephyr, rather

I am my words and my words
are me who I created so
that they might create me:

glory to life! glory to identity! glory to
the fountain pen that drips the
spilled ink of my thoughts onto
the paper and births me into existence.

Helen of Troy

She's been retired
for a while now—the whore
of Babylon finally
stoned and laid to rest
beneath the hardened sepulcher
of a bathroom sink, but

the old girl hasn't lost
the drive—even after all
the years. *Helen of Troy*
masquerades across her two-toned
prongs as the black mamba of her
cord trails in a woven mess;

what's your poison? she whispers softly
280? 330? How about 450?

Those degrees rose in cadence
with the heat of love she stripped
the innocence tangled in my follicles—
from blond to auburn to
black to brown to blond again,
each time I pass by her,
I still hear the ghost of her voice
calling to me as she says,
"Plug me in and give me a go."

She and I

We were magnets of equal polarity—
try to force us together and
we just repelled. Maybe
it was the alcohol;
we needed that to get close—
to neutralize the static
so we could touch.

Blazing green eyes burn bright
and ambition ponds in her irises
where hazel brown flakes construct an idea;
She had plans--standards she'd
set for me which felt like two kids
playing a game of keep away—one shorter,
one taller and I, the shorter.

Strands of hair mirror the aspects of
her temperament, short and
lit like a fuse. In the zone where the light
captures the frame in black and white,

I am standing in the divot;
she has a shovel in her hand,
glares of ice crystalizing tears
over allowing too much light
inside the development room
her words, an imprint, rolling through August heat:

I can't believe that you'd even call yourself my son.

The Betrayed

It's like Uncle Larry whose respect
means everything to you, calling you
"my little girl" when you're really a boy—

it's like Dick, your high school bully
following up the steps to your next class,
in pantomime of fingering you,
making sex noises and calling you a "faggot."

It's like trying to enjoy a meal at
your favorite restaurant with close friends when
you hear a confederate harlot
snickering; mocking you and
when you finally gather the balls to speak up and
take ownership in your right
just to be tolerated, she says,
"This is America—I have freedom of speech."

It's like singing your heart out in church because
music is the one thing that makes you feel like
there might just be a husk of a God above
in this world who could love you for you
when the pastor's daughter approaches you
at the benediction and says she knows
that you've been "living in sin"—

because you are the betrayed; the
accomplice of Sodom, the ally of Gomorrah.
Because you are the hollow: an akaryocite of a person,
defined by abnormal psychology as a
head case until 1973.

I could tell you it's "just a phase" or
that "it's a sin" and I
could tell you who *we* are,
but in a society that can't discern between
an Algonquian and an Aleutian, it just wouldn't matter so
instead, I'll just dip my pen into the venom of
my thoughts and curarize this world with
bisexual poison.

Identity

I fell to my knees writing poems for him *when*
I realized that every phrase and sound; all my *words*
were not my own; that this entire time I was *run—*
—ning away from myself as my identity ran *dry,*

and I could not bring the clay to the life we tried to build.
He
tried to make me his doll—and as he *does*
everything to me that I asked him *not*
his fingers lash like wind; a desperate *try*

to mold my contour to fit his form. Never again, *nor*
will he swallow me to fill a void—to *do*
so because no one can fill his vacancies better than *I.*

My soul sings a mantra: I. I am. I am, I am. And "*we*"
are not of the same unit; *are*
not of the same part or whole, riding *on*
the backs of each other to achieve some impossible *par.*

No—I am not. I am not *he*
who will give his all *just*
to pacify a conception of what "*is,*"

of what it means to be an individual and *I*
write now for me—for the glory of *just*
being able to say that I exist; that I *am.*

Repeat mantra: I am. I am. I. Am. I am fully who I want to
        be *and*

he does not have the power to create a *"we"*
out of the ashes of what used to be *just*
so the world will say, "look at what we *are*."

Hands

These hands of mine are history
recorded in the lines along my palms
and with the pen and with the paper
they will sing vivacious songs.

These hands of mine are lovely
with grace within their grip—
yet these hands of mine won't hesitate
to leave their print upon your lip.

These hands of mine are workers
who from dawn to dusk will toil
to mine the air around me
until their skin begins to boil.

These hands of mine are thinkers
grinding their cogs and gears
as they stroke a line of stubble
that turns grayer with the years.

These hands of mine are lovers
as they burn your face into my eyes
they will touch you and they'll taste you
tickling their way up through your thighs.

These hands of mine are warriors
yeah, they've broken a board or two,
yet these hands of mine are fragile
for they have been broken, too.

These hands of mine are creators
who mold the contour of this rhyme,
and these hands of mine are preservers
who battle the tides of time.

III

DARKER SHADES OF GLAM

In a Little Court of Politics

Two shaded masters stand
idle on either end; one side
arrayed in white linen. The
other side, corrupted marble—
as blind as black and twice as dark.

The round ones band together first,
a line of silent sentinels
expressions cold, emotionless
stares across the cream-speckled
marble-washed field of battle in
staking sweeps of checker-drive.

The pieces are slaughtered for purpose—
banished to the outerworld; that
mysterious realm where warriors align
like phantom trophies for the other side
in hazes of white and black
and cold-stone marble.

They are motionless, mostly, and move
only at the astral fingers of their
tacticians—unseen puppeteers on
opposing sides as the round pieces hedge
their buffer zone, caught in blade-lock
and horses fall from under their
cavaliers, crushing charge, crippling
momentum, their bones snapping as
marbled-marrow leaks from cleft wounds.

and in the end, it's all about manipulation.

checkmate.

maybe money really does grow on trees

my mother always said, "money doesn't
grow on trees," but I couldn't disagree more because
I really think it's just a matter of perception—

sometimes I walk down to Lindley Park and
I try squinting at the trees; then I try squinting harder
until the leaves change their color,

even shape. The color of the leaves merge
and darken to mimic the color of dirty bills
in the shapes of dollar signs. And sometimes

if I use my imagination, I see silhouettes of Grant
and Franklin inscribed on the foliage in droves, but
I've always been well-versed in

deluding myself. And it's relatively easy to do if
you just believe in meta-lies so much that they
morph into truths, which I guess explains why

I drink PBR from brandy sifters
and pretend these sequins are diamonds
that I wear in my dreams.

I Am Aries

I am Aries—first born, first bred
first blood and first dead who
rumbles through sticks and bramble
with head down, horns forward
and thorns in his eyes. Who

breaks forth in bluster with
fire in his loins and rage in
his brow—who stands up, chin hairs
bristling through every breath while
snorting fireballs at the opinions of
the chosen ignorant. Who

eats apart his own insides but
rises first by break of dawn to heal
and covet the lucid light,
pouring over his skin in streams of sun-fire.

I am he bathed in flame whose
sigil stems from coldest frost; who
rides a red horse to ruin, brandishing sword
high above head;

Mars his spirit—avatar of war made flesh,
patron saint of rage whose wrath
is native sin.

Nowhere

Elkin—creek-crossed basins and
bramble-snatched. humble-roots rolling
like tumble weeds in Yadkin's valley;
wish-washed bottle jars as
glass pipes clinkle-glisten in twilight's spark
at Friday night ballgames—

temper-touched in tampered-places; swallowing
grapes and snorting purple while weed-wasting,
baking by train-trestles. Clack, clack, clickity-clack—
skater boys and Marble Arches—the pulling tides of
teens and hormones through sandstone and marble blast
by ole' Vulcan's quarry;

where a blind-eyed, wound-licked drop out
opens his lids and wakes up
confused, coated in all the *cultural* colors
in a Boro of gates.

Darker Shades of Glam

its aura is a hue of faded turquoise,
that once sparkled like sequins
scattered by the light. A jolt of former

razzle-dazzle becomes the hot scent of musk
which pricks the nose like vague nostalgia,
seeped in black but overlaid in flaking gold—

the curtains are drawn back,
dyed teal, gleaming like silk,
but soiled velvet to the touch.

dappled light fills the room
from a rusted windowpane;
a dusty desk is set beneath a frail beam

of evening sun—where once a presence stood,
gazing out the aperture, calling Hollywood stars by name,
drawing fabled constellations to trace the outline

of a bleak fantasy. the stillness of the room
is troubled by the imprint of a heavy sadness
where influence infects in darker shades of glam.

A Breakfast Memorandum

for B. Pardue

A subtle stillness pervades
the moment—the sound of sweet
jazz tunes, filling the air
with you in your gym shorts,
cooking breakfast in my kitchen—
the rushing sound of water

tracing its way over
the golden hue in your skin:
what is it like to love you,
brother of mine?

I notice you more often than you think,
but some thoughts
are best left voiced
by the cracking of eggs
over the narrow edge
of my stove, and how they will soon
sizzle and pop when put
to the burner;

in the silence filling the void
where words become superfluous—
there is a beam of sunlight

caught by cigarette smoke and kitchen fumes
and in that frame, I know:
no one understands better than you.

Sister Scar:

for A. Triplette

from whom all passion flows—
in waking state
of a troubled mind.

you who should know better
yet chased the trail
of a glistening rainbow—

let the heart burn onward;
sail into that realm,
unknown and unnoticed whose

sublimity speaks in subtle
shades of deep vibration:
I call your name

on wings of fire unbending:
awake the depths of
who I am and

with the whispers on your winds—
breathe life into my veins.
Sing to me about who you are

and press onward still,
sing the sonnet of those
who stand upon the edge of the night

and sing higher far!
endure. Endure! the breath of the faithless,
not of choice but of circumstance,

then do not sink into pools
of melancholy but this—
remember.

And honor the memory of who
you were and are
and always shall be.

it's really hard to write about you

                                    for W. B. Dudley

i've been trying to write about you
for a long time, but could never fit
the letters of your name into
my poems. But that night
when we sat by the fireplace
on the patio of the Fairfield,
I remember the stiff air
serenaded our cold chills—
the funeral, the arrangements
emotions spewing like volcanoes
from our chests—our hearts were nuclear reactors.

the others could not reach you,
the others could not reach me;
but in that moment
when our timelines crossed yet again,
in the embrace that fell between us
pulling you into me; pulling me into you

i felt the world bend around us as time stopped.
and could count the minutes only
by the baseline of our hearts,
each pulse of life marked
down the second hand where winding ticks
troubled the stillness in the air
wrapping me up in you,
wrapping you up in me:

when fire met water I found healing in the steam
deep burning, quenched by the hook
of your arm; where your river had frozen,
crying tears of ice melted by my radioactive clutch;
flesh seared into flesh—

● ● ●

our bodies consumed each other
and we stood resilient to pulling away.

An elegy; in memoriam

for A. Matthews

I.

I did not have enough time
when I heard a star had fallen—
I stood in the back with clammy hands
beside a mutual friend as my
stomach churned when I heard
the words spoken at the funeral:
hushed whispers, lingering within
the long dark—

they did not know him.

He went to his grave
wrapped not by shroud but
by secrets—words uttered
and not dared spoken loudly.

II.

I met you in the heart
of a distant summer and I
knew you in the heat
of a brief summer night:

your skin against my skin,
your lips crashing wantonly
into my own, conspiring things
under the covers with me
that no eyes saw,

yet every ear in the hotel
that night heard with my

forehead fevering its way
within your blood while my bareness

entwined with your own—
I moved within you and you,
under me, panting in sweat
and blurred visions of the divine

that flashed before our eyes
as our flesh melded together
if only for a night.

III.

We did not dream
those dreams that were planned—
what did you ever know
of a piano? How deep

did the shades of ebony
and the hues of ivory
sear into your being?
did sullen musicality

fill you as much as they claimed?

I saw you play
only once—and you saw
me teach, but never.

IV.

If I am to see you again,
it comes in smell first:
salt-seared wind filtering
through my nostrils;

then comes the sounds—
infectious laughter
that burns the soul even now
in the echoes of its vibrations:

there is a gull I hear,
calling us by name
from somewhere far above—
and then I hear the waves

crashing against a well-battered
shore, and though the roar
of moist ocean wind
would cleanse everything

from the wake of my conscience,
it cannot.
I hear your voice best when I press a conch
to my ear: that is when I feel

the subtle dampness on my lobe,
and I can feel the bright sun
burning its tan into dry skin,
reminding me of your smile

in all its beauty—harbinger
of the sublime—come

to make me *feel* again.

V.

There are letters I have written
for you, still unsent
and words you would have said
to me, yet unspoken.

o, voice! o, laughter!
o, late night coffee shared! o,
smiles that passed solemnly
with hushed understanding—

I feel I know you
at your core—where others
were too afraid to go—
fear did not define us;

nor did it blind from
a conversation between the cracks
in two old souls.
What others passed as shallow,

I waded deep into its being.

VI.

Fearless soul, who in love endures;
fearless love, where heart abides;
fearless heart, that joy ensures;
fearless joy, in self, not pride—

fearless self, I love you still.
Fearless, even in face of shade—
fearlessly wrought of fearless will;
fearless in death's pools you wade.

Fearless friend of peerless might;
fearless might of tested vice,
fearless sovereign of the night,
fearless yet to roll the dice.

Fearless you were as years are long,
fearless still among pain and spite—
fearless in right, as fearless in wrong;
fearlessly you faced death's chilling bite.

VII.

I do not cry as others
cry. My tears, instead,
are stains of ink
spilled to spell out grief
and regret—

yet you already know this.
I am sorry that I
watched and did not act—
the passiveness of my troubled hand

stayed only because I did not know
in whom or what I believed—
you, however, did, didn't you?
Perhaps, then, I regret not listening.

I spill these thoughts for your
forgiveness;
that in some way the echo of
these vibrations may wing to you.

● ● ●

VIII.

I stood with you on the precipice
of a dark day
with the sun lying behind a veil
of overcast clouds in the humidity

of late July. There was screaming
and tempers flaring to rival
the temperature of the month.
I claimed to know you,

and yet did not open an arm
in the wake of your need.

I watched you that day,
drive away in heated rage,
screaming the obscenities
of a heart that was broken;

and though I heard,
I did not listen.

IX.

You called me sometime after,
confessing truths about "us"
contrived within your solitude
against our parting.

I listened, this time,
but could not understand.
We talked for hours that day
and discussed nothing of

grief or pain. And I,

at my writing desk, reclined:
imagining you in your pajamas,
bottom only with no top,

eating my words as cereal.
We talked of "what-ifs"
and of things that could
and might have been.

You laughed and said
we both were to blame,
but I knew better—
for even when you longed

for me still, I refuted
our entwinement and your company.

X.

All too often, I too,
wonder what might have been.
When I saw you years later—
your emaciated form:

eyes once lively now sullenly sunken
into the skull upon which
they call, home: I wondered
if it might have prolonged

your brief existence had I
have taken you into the bulk
of my arms and set
your heart ablaze

with my own. I wondered if
filling you with my fire

might have banked the rage
of your passion: the fury

whose vacancy you filled
with hollow sex and drugs—
the drugs did not help:
even now I wonder if I

could have loved you unconditionally,
if it would have filled you
to where you were no longer in want
of that which you never received.

XI.

The coffin was closed
and had been sealed
by your blood.
I could not trace

the wrinkles above your brow,
or run my fingers through
the tussles of your silky hair.
I could not connect

the dots of your freckled cheek
or plant a kiss upon
your stone-cold forehead.
I could not sketch your effigy

even within the shattered fragments
of memory. I would never again
run my hands upon the crease
of your neck, or knead my fingers

over your open back. I could not

scream, for the vault left
you deaf in silence absolute.
Even your cheek-to-cheek

smile—this was robbed from me.

Those who claimed you as their own
had their closure: yet mine is sealed
by the smell of dill

and stale perfume, picketed
by a grieving mass
who would not see you
through tears of twisted vision.

XII.

You understood things in me
that others did not;
I could talk about
a mountain with you

and you understood
it was not just a mountain:
that it was life itself
within the foliage of trees

or that the gleam of the evening sun
on every blade of grass
was not just a reflection
of a waning light,

but was the mirror image
of the deep conscience—
the looking glass through which
nature recorded our every action.

Often I have wished and wondered
what it would have been like
to wrestle in the grass
with you; to feel the sweet stain

of fresh dew permeating through
the pores in our skin: what my reflection
in the mirrors of your eyes
would be: to stand in the sunlight

laughing with your laugh-lines
and how they traced

back to me.

XIII.

When we were young
we spoke of death
but never understood it;
still I do not think that I do—

but when I imagine you,
winged off to worlds unknown,
I understand now
that you probably do

and still, I do not.
In that way I am jealous,
o wayward one who winds swept
into the currents of the sublime,

that you set out
to explore without me.

XIV.

O naked soul whose body sleeps
'neath mounds of earth and soils deep;
where fly you now on wings of time—
freed into the wild sublime?

I wish, I wish that I could see
through cracks of fate and destiny
and write the epic song and lore
of your last step beyond the door

from life to death and mystery:
your last deep breath in history
as you crossed into the peerless black;
into the stars that called you back—

yet my feeble mind and meager pen
can only, just barely comprehend
that you are gone and that is all,
and here I stand, feeling small:

and yet I've writ your legacy;
these vibrations bind you here to me—
so that I know, where near or far,
in my heart you remain; in my heart you are.

Nighthawks

Particles of dust flow in
from the weary glow of
vacant street lights. A
sallow beam illuminates
the inside of a dinner
around the corner where
a neon sign flashes "Phillies."

I have been here
before, my lonely
footsteps lingering towards
the narrow edge of light—
to this place where the sleepless

share their somber blues in
numbers like their own
over silent sips of coffee and
malts at midnight. They
are drifters. I have been
one of them, running together

as the vice clutches
around us in the form of
thick smog. We are here
to forget and lose our realities
within the miseries of the others.

Through with Compliments

When I gave you a compliment
you took it into your hands and
let it run like sand through
the prints in your fingers.

Twirling the compliment around
in your palms, you watched it glisten
in the sunlight; your face made me
think you were searching for
subliminal meaning—

an etching here, a carving there
like an opaque hieroglyph where
adders dance for a handful of breadcrumbs.
I watched as you took the compliment

into your mouth and rolled it over
and under your tongue as it tickled
your taste buds seemingly sour.
You tasted its every grain

and then spat it out
like a slice of stale gum
and let it pass through your ear,
skipping your brain and

right out the other; you
clearly did not value it so
next time, I'll just weave
it into the tresses of your hair and

what you feel then, will be
a sticky, gooey sensation, binding
you up in knots—the price you pay

• • •

for letting the compliment

that I gave you

go.

The Shape of Shadows

I wallow with a wolf
in the dark, alone—usually
tooth-in-neck, with fangs
splintering like shards of ivory.

the chill of his aura
is buffered by the wind
on his breath, I succumb to
his imprint which grows

like a castle of black thorns over
the light in my eyes. Yet
his sallow eyes see clearly in
the darkened corners of my

peripherals—and in my shadow
he is there. Trauma runs in rivers
of red under his razor nails and I
am expected not to ask questions,

but grit my teeth and interpret the
marks he leaves behind as maps
that lead with crimson lines to
a fabled trove of answers.

I have familiarized myself by now
with the shape of his shadow, and
I know what dark and angry contours
define his form. In the wake

of his approach, I have learned
to speak prayers in cloven tongues
of fire. And though the wolf hears
he cannot understand.

cabernet sauvignon

I have tasted heartbreak
and felt it dancing along
the tip of my tongue,
entwining around my taste buds
in a tango of knives.

I can detect its scent inside
empty wine glasses stuffed
with all the over-piled dishes
in the kitchen sink
that you left behind;

there is a pungent scent
of fermented grapes
abrasive odors of cedar,
flowers, roses perhaps—and the molded
smell of yeast decaying
in every shade of red.

I feel it most when I swallow
tracing the track of the esophagus;
a mixture that in the moment
held a torch into the sun—

It streams down the throat; a river of Novocain,
trickling through the current of the soul
into a dreamscape ocean of questions.

Here slumber is not a choice but a vow
when spoken, marries the pain—
loathsome burnings; insufferable headaches
induced by too many sulfites
dripping from the vein
of a heart that's dying.

● ● ●

The influence referendum: between Ginsberg, a coffee, and me

I

Mercury went direct. And so this is how
it begins—there is a symphony in the cosmos;
all stars murmur with vibrations; each humming
as the messenger lifts his baton and the stars sing.

Far off in the distance, a black hole whirls,
speedway of light as radiation
bursts into being. Earth too—
sings in harmony: made

of radio transmissions, or cars
speeding on broken highways;
a transfer truck screams into the night,
basso-profundo mixing with the

alto of lover's sighs and here
is Orion's forlorn face—he looks to Leo
and Regulus shrugs; it is the center of everything
and here the heart beats to the

bass of the stars. In the time lost
between the warrior's club
and the lion's maul, light streams
like a black candle, burning hotly in the night.

the light of Polaris is blocked
by a nebulous cloud and
there; farther than light can travel
and twice as fast

is the genesis of illusion.

II

Black fire! Black fire! Why do you burn?
So much darkness; what is the fabric
of the dark matter? Tell me if you can:
what are the celestial
coordinates of Oblivion?

I want to write a poem for every star,
but it is too dark; I cannot see
what lies in front of me because
I do not know it exists.

Neither did the natives; only the
shamans—who walked on both
sides—could see Columbian ripples
over the water of known infinity—
they breathed with a third eye;

and only from gunshot—sound cutting
through air; a rip from a different dimension—
did they know that life existed elsewhere
and that truth. Brought Death. On the wing.

III

i think my father fell from the sky;
a lover smacks the stratosphere
and a father hit the ground. i
imagine a belt of stars across
his waist, shimmering
like rhinestones in the heat
of photosynthesis—he has lived
billions of lives. somehow he
has seen Vega's supernova
while we were still waiting.
at most, we will see the DVR
event, because our eyes could not
make it home in time. not our
faults. just our backwards perspective;
like infants. if we cannot see it. it does not.
exist. so we hold
a conch shell to our ears and pretend
it is a cell phone; or a walky-talky
and we wonder why we cannot make
contact with those just beyond
Orion's belt. monkeys building a
tower to Mars from sticks and
stones that they use to smite
each other. the conch shell whispers though. and
they believe it is a voice. maybe it
is—it is Gaia replying:

what are you doing?

you're going to kill me.

IV

What happened on Pangaea when.
Civilizations were unified? When
everyone danced. To one beat. On one rock. What
happened to the moon? Running wild on polar winds.
Through the fur of wolves and
the blankets of the Iroquois?

Where did we lose. Live and. Let
live? When did we assume
superiority over others simply because.
We don't accept. Their way of doing things. Right?

I wanted to write a poem
about Cosmos. Why did it turn. Into
Chaos? I knew only my father
would know, but I was lost and.
Needed direction. As I tried to track. Him down. I
consulted the
Christian—he said, *don't ask. just accept.* So I spoke
to the T'aoist who said, *why does it matter?* Then I
crossed the mountains. And consulted the Cherokee. He
said:
from the sky.

It occurred to me that. No one really knows. And even
more just
did not care. Squabbling over differences
as opposed to converging over verisimilitudes.

V

Don't stop here,
the story hasn't been written;
and these words are the binary vision

through the eyes of a madman in C-minor;
there's a property of truth that
can only be heard

when the world finally
stands still. And still,
I believed Newton when

he said that the only way
to stop motion is
to use force—

imagine—

if everything just stopped
moving all at once a
              slow current first then

suddenly. Nothing.

and all the world
a frozen glacier of conventions—
the universe even; all bodies. Stopped.

Technical difficulty—oops;
there are some bugs
that God just hasn't figured out yet.

Sweet Satan child of sacrilege—
that's what the church billboard

will read next Sunday. A great

man he was, but what Einstein
didn't tell us;
hydrogen and helium really aren't the

atom bomb—oh no,
the bomb is the man
who presses the button.

Sallow-belly, dangerous general:
did you know that Hiroshima
would blend into the fabric

of your kimono?

VI

Perhaps I am not such a singularity.

We all have daddy issues—we just
never wanted to admit it; and
because we did not know a mother
could exponentially square the
number of twins inside her womb,
we never wanted to concede. To admit.

That looks are geo-formed. The sun shines on
Africa, so their skin is charred. It rises
on Asia, so their skin is yellowed
from the morning light. It sets on
Europe; which is why they are pale
and it stands at noon over America,
which is why Americans. Think that they
are always right.

Interlude

Lost.
      Fragmented.
   de-

     magnetized like

a

         w*rd.

       missing its letters. Where

   did this transmiss—

    —up wrong?

    I

cannot-connect

      these blank spaces

        too vast in light

   years apart.

where

are

we, where!

are

we?

VII

I traveled. Not knowing
what else to do
and wrote these volumes
of diaries in poetic conventions.

If I were lost, I'd choose
to forget myself within
the great Navajo Desert—
that is where I went
to lose myself on a surface
like Mars because all I knew
was that. This is where Ziggy
was from. And an Aries—Martian of
spirit. Would be out of
my miseries in a place
to remind me of what I thought
was home.

Great red ball of dirt
in the sky—shimmering
with the rust of years;
icy and cold without affection
from the sun. It made

the most sense—war is man's
common ancestor; the only thing
we must be—child of Ares—god of
war. Named Mars. Because we
cannot agree—great ram of fire
who would split open the sky;
agent of Chaos and here
my father lies.

VIII

At the end of my rope
in a hopeless quest,
I remember sitting
about a bonfire. The
air of a desert night
is frigid. Arizona ice—
like polar caps teasing bare skin.

I danced with my ancestors—
savages that lived since
the sky had formed;
we sang in vibrations incomprehensible
though we knew what the other
meant.

In that lonely hour, where
hope froze like a Canadian river,
my eyelids lifted to the
great dome above and

I saw.

IX

We are not one;
ignition was jammed

and something failed to click:
just ghosts in the shell

matchlock is too wet,
but I can still smell

the gunpowder—I hate

how it lingers

in a thick haze over the head;
gaskets are blowing and

my chest is feeling like
led—in my throat there are

gumballs buzzing as they circle the machine;
and finally blue becomes less of a color

and more of a feeling. Fading just a moment
it swallows itself like rocks rolling

through the trachea-track, the knife's edge;
jagged blade pioneering through my gut.

I lost my voice when
I heard the gun fire

and started screaming into the dark,
praying that someone could hear

then red. Red. All is read
like the page of a Marquis.

Where did the world run
when fire reigned from the sky?

X

Ten. Ten systems. Ten journeys.
Tens of thousands of
zeroes and ones. Ten being

the beginning ten
being the end. Ten ships still
have to sail. And ten

heroes still sit around
the decagon of Ormen
where ten black candles

burn in ten plumes of flame
and in the center—just one.
One being "The One" when

paired from *the* absolute,
the Oblivion, *the* zero, *the*
nothingness; one and

zero making ten. And here,
the timeline of infinity endlessly
repeating in clusters of ten,

learning ten lessons that
they did not see ten times infinity years ago
when they committed the original ten sins.

And here tens upon tens upon tens
of decades lifted to the tenth degree
cycling upon a perfect zero—

infinite loop; eternal continuum
encapsulating the imperfections of one

* * *

because he is not ten.

X-i

Here is the wormhole of Eden—
how else might a snake
slither inside? At this auspicious place,
where dynasties disappear and gravity

crushes its weight even against itself,
there is a low fog kissing
the morning of the day
upon the soles of the innocent who live within.

A gate greets the intruder
as the dimensions of their being distort;
scrambling their matter to be
reassembled elsewhere---as a different person,

body; soul, even. And yet crawling
in our BDUs, we blend upon
the deep green, we seethe as a sleek bleed
underneath it all; unnoticed—not yet detected.

Women are dancing naked in an ivory-upon-ivy
courtyard. Here the landscape is
a dream—too surreal to be written and
too opaque to be sketched; low clouds

are hanging overhead where lightning
unceasingly rages, yet never strikes the ground.
We are hot and raw, beads of sweat propelled
by a scorching flame squelching from the gorge.

Our gaze is averted, our ears pulled from the alluring
beat of an exotic drum. Voices cry out
down a narrow corridor and we
do not know if in agony or ecstasy. Bones

* * *

crunch underneath us yet the expedition goes on
and suddenly sand; legions of sand—forming
a vacuous pit as it swallows all. Two of us die
while one turns back; then there is I.

Just I. A singularity churning slowly
in my solidarity down the drain. The dim
light of the dark hallway is eclipsed
and I am swallowed by the blind black.

I see and hear nothing. Nothing but
the endless eons of the crackle;
granular sand—running in a river.
Moments later, I am falling

and still seeing nothing I
fall endlessly; lurch in the gut
upheaval of all with my blood
not knowing in which direction to flow.

X-ii

As I fell through the fabric of Oblivion,
I could finally see, while still falling,
only now my feet fell first.

I am seeing the universe as a recording,
the great lie is that everything is real.
Here are the archives of Arcturia—

and Arcturus, the great librarian of it all;
each image playing on demand, all around me
as I fall. I see the smile of Adrienne

• • •

and Ginsberg salutes me on my way down.
Waldrop peddles on a bicycle, following
me as I plummet through the void.

I can see Whitman laughing and I
am hearing the sobs of Plath.
Dickenson exchanges a knowing glance

and Shakespeare is playing guitar
in a party hat. And still I see more:
Frost is preaching about the world's end

and Eliot is dancing naked around a cactus.

X-iii

The farther I fell, the further I see:
I know well by now what comprises my exoskeleton;
it seems as though I am falling into myself
where stanzas cease dividing and my life—so linear

   —all becomes one sentence united into a vignette of
my mother's face; I think I have finally made her proud and
dad isn't drinking half as much anymore: I can only
conclude that this is a dream, though their faces are so clear
that I could reach out and touch them—something is
moving on the inside, perhaps it is the flake of the
encrusted obsidian that Sheratan's electricity had contoured
around my core; and Hamal, my brightest star blazing like
a dagger of flame, straight into the root of it all—that yes,
now I see:
*I have been young for too long and became old way too
soon* and so the days pass on in a flash of lightning; too
quickly to see how beautiful it all actually is and I saw
myself growing up and, at times, struggled to recall the
scenes firing off in flashes from a cinema reel; who was I
when I wanted to fall in love, I found myself aching—
perhaps then a boy, and only in pain could I learn to be a
man; then
to see my diaries and each poem, a letter never sent, that's
when I could hear the words in a sonic boom of my
frustrations, splattered across the pages—man was I mad,
my diction breathing out the poison of my thoughts and the
corruption of a misguided will and all the times I tried to
run and stumbled over my own feet, shielded from the fall
only from the grace that pulsed within Mesarthim's wings
—noble phoenix, so far away—luminary of my path; not
even Polaris had the power to guide me through flipping
burgers at a convenient store just to pay for my rite to
survive; I swear by the dust in my bones that I

• • •

swatted away my uncle's hand just as I was passing into that deeper, arctic region.

X-iv

Here is a radio transmission bursting
through this reverent introspection and

as the vortex spirals on, I catch
only the end of it: "10-4

good buddy! I can read you loud,
but not clear." I must have

overheard God's freightmen as the cosmic
winds began whirling past me. It

is growing cold and the embers of
the burning rush now feel

like a broken heat unit in the middle
of a frigid day. My heart

is beginning to slow; my body,
a comet, and while my tail

blazes with radiation, I feel
ice crystals forming around my core

as if to cushion an impending impact.
The ache has seeped now into green pools

and has settled now
into my lower diaphragm;

it is hard to breathe. I am just now
realizing that I am not afraid—

there is no solid ground to be seen

• • •

and yet, in concession

of a system failure, I begin
to feel Mesarthim, merging

feathers of fire into my back;
wings sprouting like vines

and though I can fly,
the updraft is too strong,

so I push myself down
to grind upon the grain of the wind.

This is the realm where my friends dwell;
where I can see the raw separate themselves

from the fabled constants. Multiplying
and dividing, they merge with my aura in 4D;

around me, they assemble a coat
made of ice yet harder than diamond.

The jobs that I've carried,
anchor weights of the ship,

swirl in a heated blaze,
constitution of my tail.

And so here they are and
I can see them as blocks—

moving through life, transcending death,
warranting that I have enough.

X-v

And so I fell through desire;
rumbling pyre burning like blue-bell flame;
spreading its way throughout the nerves,

up the track of the stomach
where it confiscates the heart.
Here, the air is humming softly—

every atom is bouncing from wall to wall
just to try and stay warm.
There are

snowflakes here and yet
they will disappear, burning long before
they are able to reach

whatever lies below, and I,
like those snowflakes in hot pursuit,
reckless heat, chasing a holy grail:

Below me, I can finally see a sea
and in the reflection where the light
bends low upon its surface, I view

the faces of my lovers past,
shimmering over the murky deep;
yet from my height,

that which is far away
emits the illusion of intimacy.
Each of their eyes

supernovae of feeling

● ● ●

exploding over the surface of my brain.
My heart seizes in tantrum-rage

and I want—
squinting eyes and gritting teeth:
my armor of diamond clutches

tightly around me, preparing the inevitable.
A tidal wave churns eastward
from below—something is disturbed from the deep.

X-vi

Here is the netherworld;
the land where the human mind
sinks low into the base
of consciousness—where reason

is eclipsed and passion
rules the impulses that
lie beneath. Primal sub-terrain
where the water is cold,

displaced in composition, breaking
even; absorbed by the pores
enumerating my skin. SOS—
there is a chink in the armor

and I am drowning;
here the words of the wise
are swallowed and distorted
before sound can penetrate the brain;

misunderstanding flows in currents
of mercury, running retrograde.
Speaking is impossible, for I do not have gills—

hearing, negatory—laughing at a foreigner

to fill the vacancy of what the mind
did not receive. Receptors shut
down and the great eye closes—fabricating
an illusion to follow in absolute absence.

A compass is spinning; haywire.
The voice speaks erelong; it is I
who chooses not to listen. At this apex
of being, the lover and the monster converge.

Beneath this water, the compass freezes
and the deeper I swim
the more lost I become. Here, I
am not one, but now two—

perhaps three or four. I dive
so much deeper—so deep
that my helmet begins to crack,
knowing confidence as my enemy.

—*open your eyes*—

instead of feigning peace through aversion;
and as this voice screams, it penetrates
the leagues of water-weight.
Glossy eyes open from the deep black

and the pitch is replaced; then bubbles!
all is bubbular, and I, a bubble
too. Like fissures boiling low
within Mariana's womb, I see them rise,

each face, a hornet in swarm,
vying to touch their lips to mine.

I heard them try to speak—but this
is Neptune's realm where water

swallows sound, gargling is native tongue,
and without sight, the mind sketches.
The gaseous bubbles of faces past
ignited in the shimmering light and formed

a shape that I believed
to be a rose—and each petal
arose within itself, an intricate web
all arisen—resin of arsenic.

A rose for each lover.

X-vii

Judge me not harshly
by the truth concealed herein:
a rose for you all.

VITAE ET AMORIS
*****
*

From spring of life forged
we youthful lover's passion:
Naive eyes of love.

*

Your unrequited
love. Too afraid to let live,
Too afraid to die.

*

First time my heart fell:
T'was grown in the wrong season;
Life got in the way.

*

Drawn to each by art,
Your pictures, my stage display:
But just could not spark.

*

A ghastly mistake,
forged of arrogant hubris--
made me lose it all.

*

Hardly worth pen-stroke:
Desire as deep as your skin.
Languishing regret.

*

A guilty pleasure
on a hot summer day's end--
with fire in your thighs.

● ● ●

*

Crazy days wrapped in
a haze. Time ceased its meaning:
My innocence lost.

*

Unfinished business,
all too quickly consumed:
Lingering remorse.

*

From false grounds was forged
by desire. One shouldn't
want what they can't have.

*

Just one drunken night;
one taste left me craving more--
but you would not give.

*

The first time I tried:
But my heart was locked away
and could not be yours.

*

Spontaneous lust
on your luxurious couch.
I did not look back.

• • •

*

To use your love was
my only aim. Wrapped in me
you became. I left.

*

A webb'd entangle:
Back and forth, forth and back we
went. I got too tired.

*

Just an outlet that
I sought. A mutual use;
just an easy lay.

*

Curiosity
got my betterment. Strangers
to each other's world.

*

What a tangled web
we wove! But I mangled your
heart. You became wise.

*

We shared the stage and
played our little games to what
end? Just to pass time.

• • •

*

A chance encounter
over some jewelry. And yet
you were too forward.

*

My heart fell twice and
you were two. And left me here
in Savannah Rain.

*

A sunny day by
my pool. Apprehension drew
me under its wings.

*

A longing desire
from days long past; my failed aims
to force love to last.

*

Charming as music,
so I danced to your tune and
woke to a monster.

*

I chose you because
I was feeling so alone.
Never in good sense.

• • •

*

A dreamy summer
day. Like a holiday in
Bali. Fleeting waves.

*

Two people alone
to seek love from the lonely
and still you are here.

*

When passion runs cold,
I know you are here for me,
proving yourself o'er.

*

Like man's greatest fall:
so was mine for you. Purest
love; how did it fail?

X-viii

In a fulminating cloud, here in the deep
the rose flashed and they sang a chorus—

dissipating each, one by one; vacuumed
upwards towards a shimmering surface

they continued to sing, "Forget me not!"
and so my eyes pulled the petals, one by one

and I knew I could question why some things worked
and other things didn't, but I knew that was not

the final leg of this journey. No. As the rose cloud
seeped like red ink into the water, merging with

hydrogen and oxygen, I saw a flare from below:
origin of want from lover's past. Here was

a great fissure—divide in the ocean's floor
where heat erupted in a storm of bubbles so

I swam into the fissure;
great divide—window into Terra's womb.

I saw within a glimpse of true shade:
burnt orange—blood of the earth, rising—

the deepest fathom of desire
is the orange glow—heat

in the core of its icy exterior
that the whole world covets

but no one possesses a pick strong enough:

* * *

on my way inside this oil well of life

I can hear saints chanting
as I penetrate the viscous pyroclasm

magma flows over my form,
and my body is encased

by the placenta of genesis.
Here I become an embryo,

nourished by the liquid fire, revived
by Gregorian hymns. Her entrance

is spirituality incarnate and
I am reminded of what I want;

a home, a love, a job, a dream; a statue
that will stand long after my decay.

Losing myself in the sensualities
of the eternal, and in one

great upheaval that makes
my limbs quake; breath belabored:

I find my death within her.
Contraction of the unknown—tension

in eternal release; joining who I am
with where I want to be,

I feel the life leave my eyes, eyes
roll back, electricity becomes the current

commanding my blood to course and I

• • •

know no more. No more than I

cannot find the will to withdraw;
eyes open now—and clairvoyance.

I stand here, facing my own ego.
There is a bookshelf—a matrix: great library

within the deep mantle. And each word spans
the books, reading like a road sign in motion.

I have arrived inside origin and I am seeing
that the only merit of my existence

is ink. Every drop of ink—
my essence. And my all—that I could ever spill.

X-ix

I know now that I have reached the root
of genesis. Before me, gaseous balls
of light fulminate above the narrow edge

and some stone of which I do not know
pads my soles and each echo of my footfall
is a narrative archived by this temple.

I trace my glide after the free-forming light,
past two archaic doors—gates
leading into the point of beginning.

In here there are whispers
falling into the tones of a celestial language
and I lose my breath, my words in a vacuum;

mind synapses misfire. Cerebral attack.
Eyes blind, but vision is clear.
Before me is a tree,

spanning a distance greater
than the farthest star.
It has red foliage that never browns

and mighty limbs that breathe
but never bend or bow.
Its trunk twists round and round—

infinite spiral, invariable helix wrought
with perfection and mutation alike;
innumerable strands upon strands and between them

vacancies that nothing in creation is great enough
to fill. Here are the secrets of the ages

• • •

from which all creation stirs

to draw breath. And I, so weak; so lowly,
diamond shell glistening undetectable
within the gaseous light—standing

beneath its towering frame. Arc of life.
Root of all. Genesis of Identity. DNA
of the universe—am I finally home?

X-x

Between the Transits that I spanned—passing through
cosmic dust; reposing within the eye of the cyclonic chaos
constituting my Identity—coating myself in defense: these
are the Darker Shades that paint my peripherals. I
contoured well in camouflage—crawling through the belly
of Eden, and the black fires of Ormen—passing through
death, searing flames and arctic waters; crossing oceans of
stars and all to find my progenitor.

I saw the balls of gas converging at the base of the tree;
colliding together, they formed the silhouette of a man who
had no face; no one form or frame. I knew then, this was
my father—his voice boomed across the hinges of stone
and I heard him say that he is only an illusion that I created
to assign myself a sense of purpose.

I wanted to cry. I wanted to scream into the narrow
corridors of Oblivion, enshrouding me now like a fog of
destiny. That at this one pivotal point in the center of the
universe where the tree of life never sheds its plumes, I
finally found what I was looking for—only to realize that it
does not exist. In hysterics, brine seeped from my eyelids
and I looked at him—the man with no face—and all I could
do was choke back that which is now wasted water. I shook
my head, sighed. I laughed. And smiling, I said, *I finally
get that now*.

He said the greatest irony in the world is that everyone
wants to be remembered when the only memory that exists
is their own. He said everyone wants to know how we came
to be. That there is no "we" really—only "I." He said listen
up because this is a proverb—there is no we, only I—there
is no I—only we. Got it? I nodded. He told me the most
important thing of all is that the word "I" can be connected

to the linking verb "am" to form "I am." This, he said, is why you exist. And this, alone, keeps you existing.

And all the fabled "we"—organisms terrified of extinction assimilating in fear to form a colony that will survive. My father told me then there is no greater fear than death because we have loved life too fondly; we fuck to ensure our name goes on: and this name only a word; murmured vibration in a sea of sounds, and if you listen closely you'll hear the conscience form a thought: it grabs a subject, contracts a verb and an adverb, conjures a transitive verb, and then silences everything with an infinitive verb:

"I don't want to die."

The truth, he said, is that we fabricate a reality and shape it with the fumes of ambition. We hold to that gumption and ride it out until we have consumed everything and have nothing left to contribute. On the scale of infinity, he said, the persistence of memory is little more than a Dali painting. And yet what is memory but a hologram recorded by the eyes and saved by the brain; forced by age into the recesses, great biological storage cloud of a mechanism that savors what it wants and deletes the rest?

And here is time, my father said as he pointed up. And upwards I saw a river running like the Milky Way—slow, smooth, steady and everything in the universe moved with it. The authority that even stars cannot withstand—only a stream flushing about a great drain; and even time is lost on itself, like me, though never frantic, always steady. Always. Self-assured.

And as I wept before my illusory progenitor, I lifted my eyes into the cosmos and just above the tree's scarlet

● ● ●

foliage, I saw. Everything moved, motion eternal, and at the epicenter of the swirl of it all—it bled over into one.

Epilogue

On the continuum of infinity

why do I fear falling

if I feel I cannot land?

www.ingramcontent.com/pod-product-compliance
Lightning Source LLC
Chambersburg PA
CBHW061151040426
42445CB00013B/1648